This is not a revision buddy that fits easily each topic you need t

CW00919972

Each topic includes b the chances of gettin

Each summary includes a code you can scan with your phone to expand your revision, online.

Some ways to improve learning and recall

☑ Don't forget that we all have our own ways of learning. Experiment to find your best ways

☑ Don't mind making a fool of yourself, either! All that matters is that it works for you

☑ Studies have shown that you learn best when you have hourly breaks, and do something completely different, particularly involving physical exercise

Organise yourself and others

☑ Reduce all your notes into short and precise bullet points

Multi-sensory approach

☑ Write out your notes and then trace them over with a finger

☑ Say them out loud to yourself

☑ Cover them up one line at a time, and see if you can remember them, and make the sections bigger each time

☑ Try singing your notes to a favourite tune and the words may stick by association

Learn to Revise

Build your confidence

☑ Say out loud that you can remember all these notes and will amaze people. "I am the best!"

Teach yourself

☑ Imagine teaching these notes to your friends and family, making it simple and interesting

☑ Try speaking them in your head, and then speaking them out loud

☑ After this, sit alone, quietly, without a phone, for at least half an hour

☑ Then repeat the exercise of speaking your notes from memory, and then repeat it the next day. See if you can remember it all one week later

Teach others

☑ Teach your fellow students. Their reactions and questions will reinforce your knowledge and help your understanding

☑ This can also build your confidence!

Overview

☑ A hedonic theory - pleasure is the key motivator and goal

☑ Based on a seven-fold calculation acronym **PRRICED** (two Rs)

☑ Pushpin is as good as poetry - no higher and lower pleasures

☑ Everyone's hedons have equal value (the Queen or me)

☑ A maximising theory - maximises welfare for the maximum number of people

☑ Works well looking backwards eg calculating social evil of backstreet abortions - a way of testing legislation against the common good rather than class interests

Key Terms

CONSEQUENTIALISM	*Assessing likely consequences for pleasure/pain*
GREATEST HAPPINESS PRINCIPLE	*Good actions maximise greatest happiness for greatest number*
HEDONIC CALCULUS	*Calculation of pleasure by hedons*
TELEOLOGICAL	*Goodness depends on end*

Bentham

Meaning

☑ There is one intrinsic good - pleasure

☑ Pleasure can be measured empirically (scientifically)

☑ Autonomy - Everyone chooses own good

☑ Equality is a radical, democratic idea

Bonus Points

☑ Economists use the theory of Marginal Utility

☑ Enlightened man becomes economic man - consuming and being satisfied

☑ Enlightenment moves ethically in two directions; Kant (deontology) and Utilitarian (teleology)

☑ Radicalism of utilitarian ethics drove social reform

☑ Democratic - everyone's happiness vote counts equally

Scan me
for more help

Or type **i-pu.sh/S9Z29C12** into your browser

Overview

☑ A maximising theory - maximises welfare for the maximum number of people

☑ Pleasures are different - higher (music) and lower (bodily eg sex)

☑ The person who's experienced both is the only person who can judge

☑ Happiness includes pleasure, right expectations, and being active not passive

☑ Two levels - Rules are given by social experience as maximising pleasure, but can be broken when a difficult choice arises/ utilitarian case for assessing the act - Mill is a weak rule utilitarian. Argues justice is a key part of social utility - we are miserable without it

☑ Motivated by virtue of sympathy for fellow human beings

Key Terms

HAPPINESS	*"Few and transitory pains, many and various pleasures and predominance of the active over the passive."* Mill
RULE UTILITARIANISM	*Utility maximised by following rules*
QUALITATIVE PLEASURE	*Higher (superior, intellectual) pleasures and lower (inferior, bodily)*

Mill's Rule Utilitarianism

Meaning

☑ **WEAK RULE UTILITARIANISM** - rules are not hard and fast (develop and can be broken)

☑ **MULTILEVEL** - generally follow a rule until a dilemma emerges - then calculate as an act utilitarian. Rights are important as guarantee of social happiness (eg rule of law)

Bonus Points

☑ Some similarities with the intuitionism of **WD** Ross (prima facie duties which can be broken)

☑ Mill influenced by Aristotle - so ends up with happiness closer to eudaimonia than to Bentham's hedonism

☑ 'Rule utilitarianism' never used by Mill - introduced by **JO URMSON** in 20th C

Scan me
for more help

Or type **i-pu.sh/S0V97G27** into your browser

Singer's Preference Utilitarianism

Overview

☑ Singer follows Hare in arguing for Preference Utilitarianism

☑ Preferences and interests are key to moral goodness

☑ Interests of the tracing Africans are as important as mine - so we should reallocate income and wealth

☑ Only reason and "sense of a future" gives you full personhood rights

☑ Abortion and infanticide are allowable

☑ Animals have personhood rights as beings with interests

Key Terms

INFANTICIDE   *The killing of infants*

PREFERENCE   *Utility is maximised by aggregating first choices*

UNIVERSAL VIEW   *Everyone's interests are assessed equally (no special cases for children etc)*

Singer's Preference Utilitarianism

Meaning

☑ Singer has been banned from speaking in Germany because of his views on infanticide

☑ He gives away 30% of his income every year

☑ No absolute rights or wrongs

Strengths

⊕ **RADICAL** - Committed to real equality

⊕ **ANIMAL RIGHTS** - Taken seriously

⊕ **SIMPLE** - Ask people what they prefer

Weaknesses

⊖ **IMMORAL** - Infanticide seems to cross a line

⊖ **IMPLAUSIBLE** - Too much to expect people not to prefer eg own children

⊖ **UNREALISTIC** - How do we calculate preferences? Or consequences?

Scan me
for more help

Or type **i-pu.sh/G4G22V37** into your browser

Overview

☑ A teleological theory (telos = eudaimonia) with deontological implications (law)

☑ We align our rational wills to the higher law of God

☑ Motivated by synderesis we pursue rational ends or primary precepts (acronym **POWER**)

☑ Then we apply them as secondary principles (eg do not abort)

☑ Primary precepts are absolute, secondary precepts are not (may change with reason and social conditions)

☑ We observe a posteriori human beings pursuing these rational ends

☑ We make mistakes and pursue apparent goods - but we never knowingly sin (genocide can be an apparent good)

Key Terms

A POSTERIORI	*From experience*
EUDAIMONIA	*Goal of flourishing*
PRIMARY PRECEPTS	*Goods observable from nature and proper purpose*
SYNDERESIS	*Humans innately want to "do good and avoid evil"*

Aquinas

Meaning

☑ Greeks saw natural law produced by proper purpose (final cause)

☑ Aquinas argues this is designed by God

☑ Four laws: **ETERNAL LAW** (divine blueprint); **DIVINE LAW** (Bible); **NATURAL LAW** (in nature); **HUMAN LAW** (legal codes)

☑ Aim is to align these four laws to produce personal and social flourishing

☑ "Natural law is the sharing in the eternal law by intelligent creatures." Aquinas

☑ Veritatis Splendor - gives a tough (absolute) statement of **NL** in response to Situation Ethics

Strengths

➕ **AUTONOMOUS** and **RATIONAL** - View of the world which infers purpose - doesn't need God necessarily

➕ **EXALTED** view of human beings - proper function to reason well

➕ **FLEXIBLE** - Secondary precepts can be altered (Aquinas takes a different view to Veritatis Splendor)

Weaknesses

➖ **FIXED HUMAN NATURE** - Is assumed. What about gays?

➖ **OPTIMISTIC VIEW** - We by nature want to "do good and avoid evil". Do we?

➖ **IMMORAL OUTCOMES** - Some interpretations ban contraception even in **HIV** riddled Africa

Scan me
for more help

Or type **i-pu.sh/N1B31W15** into your browser

Overview

☑ The natural law contains universal ideas known by intuition that "order human life and human community."

☑ There is a common process of reasoning which define "sound thinking."

☑ The theory is teleological as there is one shared end - eudaimonia

☑ The end is completed by following the seven basic goods: life, knowledge, play, aesthetic experience, friendship, practical wisdom and religion

☑ These basic goods are all equally valid - there is no hierarchy of goods

Key Terms

FIRST PRINCIPLE OF REASON	*Good is to be done and evil avoided*
FIRST PRINCIPLE OF MORALITY	*Only choose those actions compatible with human fulfilment*
BASIC GOODS	*Seven rational ends that human beings pursue*
TELEOLOGICAL	*A theory of goodness linked to ends*
UNIVERSAL	*Shared by everyone at any time of history*

Finnis

Meaning

☑ Finnis develops and uses Aquinas' first principle of synderesis

☑ Instead of the primary precepts (Aquinas) we have the seven basic goods

☑ These natural goods (or ends) are reflected in law and morality

☑ Finnis adds "play" and "practical reasonableness" to Aquinas' list and omits "reproduction."

☑ Eudaimonia is enriched by the idea of adopting a life plan

Strengths

✚ **TELEOLOGICAL** - We must commit to a fulfilling life plan

✚ **CLARITY** of the goal - Human fulfilment

✚ **COMMUNITY** - A model of morality based on the common good

Weaknesses

⊖ **CONFLICTS** - Cannot be resolved between the basic goods

⊖ **NO WAY OF JUDGING** - By practical reason between different life plans

⊖ **IMPRACTICAL** - Life plans must involve a hierarchy of goods - as these goods conflict (play versus religion etc)

Scan me
for more help

Or type **i-pu.sh/W0S09J56** into your browser

Overview

☑ Morality exists in the noumenal world of ideas like cause and effect, space and time

☑ The autonomous, rational individual can generate synthetic a priori maxims

☑ The only motive that is good is obeying the moral law as something that fills us with wonder. Duty for duty's sake - not experience

☑ Categorical Imperative has three formulations:

>☑ Universalise your Action

>☑ Universalise your common Humanity (people as ends not just means)

>☑ Universalise your position as Law maker (autonomous)

☑ The summum bonum is a mixture of virtue and happiness guaranteed in heaven for those who obey the moral law out of duty. Kant's three postulates: autonomy, immortality, God

Key Terms

A PRIORI	*Before experience, using pure reason alone*
AUTONOMY	*Freedom to make the moral law yourself*
CATEGORICAL	*Absolute command*
NOUMENAL REALM	*Realm of ideas alone*
SUMMUM BONUM	*The greatest good - a mixture of virtue and happiness*
SYNTHETIC	*Provable true or false*

Deontology

Meaning

☑ Kant enthrones autonomous rationality

☑ Radical - Each one of us can make the moral law

☑ Duty - Idea of doing something irrespective of feelings or self-interest

☑ Motive - Love of the moral law and the idea of a summum bonum

☑ God comes in to guarantee justice and happiness after death

☑ "The only good thing is the good will." Kant

Strengths

☑ **CONSISTENCY** - Goodness doesn't have special cases

☑ **DIGNITY** - Formula of Humanity guarantees rights/dignity

☑ **REASONABLE** - Universalising is what most people do. Enlightenment motto "dare to reason"

Weaknesses

☑ **INFLEXIBLE** - What happens when you have to lie to save a friend?

☑ **UNREALISTIC** - Ignores emotion. What of sympathy?

☑ **IDEALISTIC** - Attached to an idea of pure reason which doesn't exist

Scan me
for more help

Or type **i-pu.sh/F7W14D24** into your browser

Overview

☑ Summum bonum is the fruit of obedience to the moral law

☑ Moral law is discovered by a priori reason - a process of universalisation

☑ Every human being has the dignity given by reason to discover the moral law

☑ Moral law should be obeyed categorically - irrespective of feelings

☑ Duties can be perfect (contradictions in nature) or imperfect (contradictions of will)

Key Terms

CATEGORICAL   *Unconditional, absolute*

HYPOTHETICAL   *Conditional, relative*

SUMMUM BONUM   *The greatest good, a mixture of virtue and happiness*

POSTULATE   *Assumption (Kant has three - autonomy, immortality and God)*

Summum bonum

Meaning

☑ There are three versions of the Categorical Imperative: formula of law, humanity and autonomy

☑ We do our "duty for duty's sake" because by following duty we guarantee a better world

☑ We "make the law for ourselves" - autonomy

☑ The moral law within causes "wonder" as it's accessible to everyone by reason and all can help build the summum bonum

☑ **CONTRADICTION IN NATURE** - Self-contradictory for everyone to break a promise

☑ **CONTRADICTION IN WILL** - You couldn't want a world where no-one helped their neighbour

Strengths

➕ **RATIONALITY** of the summum bonum

➕ **CONSISTENCY** of our rational morality

➕ **EQUALITY** as everyone helps build the greater good

Weaknesses

➖ **ASSUMES** God is needed to guarantee it

➖ **PURE REASON** isn't as pure as Kant thinks

➖ **AUTONOMY** is a myth

Scan me
for more help

Or type **i-pu.sh/N6J91G84** into your browser

Overview

A teleological theory (telos = agape love).

Lies between legalism and antinomianism (existentialism).
Fletcher calls it "principled relativism."

We take decisions situationally.

☑ **PRAGMATIC** - Case by case

☑ **POSITIVIST** - We convert to the cause of love

☑ **PERSONAL** - The individual's needs come first

☑ **RELATIVIST** - Everything except love is relative to consequences

Six fundamental principles include "love is justice distributed" and "the means justifies the end, nothing else".

A Christian ethic - Was Jesus a situationist? Woman caught in adultery, (John 8)

Key Terms

AGAPE	*Unconditional sacrificial love*
FOUR WORKING PRINCIPLES	*Pragmatism, Personalism, Relativism, Positivism*
POSITIVISM	*Love has to be committed to before it can be realised*

Christian Ethics

Meaning

☑ Relativist in the sense that it refers to situation and consequences

☑ Absolute in the sense that there is one absolute - love

☑ Places the individual and need at the centre

☑ Fundamentally opposed to legalism eg Natural Law

Bonus Points

☑ Pope Benedict attacked the "tyranny of relativism."

☑ **RC** Church sees **SE** as the enemy of God-given Natural Law

☑ Veritatis Splendor (1995) is a very rigid interpretation of **NL** in reaction to **SE**

☑ Bishop Robinson "Honest to God" echoes **SE**

☑ Parable of Good Samaritan (Luke 22) could be a **SE** story

Scan me
for more help

Or type **i-pu.sh/G9N40Z22** into your browser

Overview

☑ Situation Ethics gives us a "terrifying degree of freedom."

☑ Clear rules and guidelines give us security

☑ Without love, freedom becomes selfishness

☑ We engage in a process of learning good habits by following rules

☑ Rules reflect the past wisdom of society

Key Terms

PERMISSIVE SOCIETY   *One in which any behaviour is permitted*

LEGALISM   *Following rules without applying reason*

WORKING PRINCIPLES   *Four basic principles of Situation Ethics*

Barclay's Critique

Meaning

Barclay gives five reasons for holding on to laws:

- ☑ Law is based on social wisdom

- ☑ Law translates into social disciplines

- ☑ Law clearly defines what is right and wrong

- ☑ Law discourages people from committing moral wrongs

- ☑ Law protects society from selfish individualism

"Freedom and law go hand in hand. By the influence of law people learn to be free."

Bonus Points

☑ Barclay concludes - if we were all saints, **SE** would be a perfect ethic.

☑ Barclay echoes the concerns of the Roman Catholic Church.

☑ Pope Benedict spoke of "the tyranny of relativism."

☑ Papal encyclicals like Veritatis Splendor (1995) reaffirm the importance of law and of absolutes.

☑ The Church argues law has an objective basis in the flourishing human life as designed by God.

Scan me
for more help

Or type **i-pu.sh/C0N49W71** into your browser

Overview

☑ Judith Jarvis Thompson - Violinist analogy, Woman's right not to have her choices violated

☑ To be forced to stay attached to dependent being is "outrageous."

☑ Mary Anne Warren - "A foetus is a human being who is not yet a person, so cannot have full moral rights."

☑ Criteria for personhood include self-consciousness, reason, communication, self-awareness

☑ **RC** Natural Law view - at conception foetus has full human rights

☑ Liberal Protestant view - abortion permitted under restricted circumstances - "Human life is sacred from its very inception."

☑ Marquis argues most abortions are "seriously immoral." Abortion denies the foetus a "valuable future like ours" - a form of potentiality argument

Key Terms

DOUBLE EFFECT	*If primary intention is good (save a life) is it morally acceptable that secondary effect is evil (foetus dies)?*
PERSONHOOD	*Issue of moral status of foetus (human, or less?)*
SANCTITY OF LIFE	*Life is sacred and inviolable*
QUICKENING	*Movement of foetus in womb at around 100 days*
QUALITY OF LIFE	*Issues of personal pain and purpose*
VIABILITY	*Ability to survive outside womb*

Abortion

Meaning

☑ Personhood implies we grant foetus certain rights based on characteristics (eg feels pain, looks human) or potentiality (fulfilled life) or because God "formed us in our mother's womb" (Psalm 139)

☑ Personhood issues are irrelevant to Thompson - it's a women's rights issue

☑ Fletcher describes unwanted pregnancy as "a form of assault on the woman."crowning jewel of God's creation

Bonus Points

☑ Singer argues children gain full personhood rights "at about four weeks" and so infanticide is morally permissive where quality of life is poor or you can replace an unhappy (suffering) child with a happier child

☑ 1990 legal term changed from 28 weeks to 24 weeks

☑ Viability is now 23 weeks

Scan me
for more help

Or type **i-pu.sh/V6B94K67** into your browser

Overview

☑ **RIGHTS** - Terry Pratchett argues for a right to choose your own death. Diane Pretty European Court case 2002

☑ **UTILITY** - Over 65s will make up 22% of the population by 2050 - Increased burden on tax revenue without quality of life. Eliminate suffering of those with dementia etc.

☑ **QUALITY OF LIFE** - Dr Anne Chapman chose to go to Dignitas, Switzerland to avoid progressive illness including loss of use of limbs and speech

☑ **SLIPPERY SLOPE** - Slippery slope argument that old and sick will be under pressure to choose to die - general rights will thereby be eroded

☑ **HOSPICE ARGUMENT** - Pain can be managed, quality protected

Key Terms

SANCTITY OF LIFE	*Life is sacred and inviolable*
QUALITY OF LIFE	*Issues of pain and purpose*
ACTIVE EUTHANASIA	*Active intervention to kill*
PASSIVE EUTHANASIA	*Allowing PVS patients to die naturally by switching off Life Support Machines*
ASSISTED SUICIDE	*A form of active, voluntary euthanasia*

Euthanasia

Meaning

☑ 1961 Suicide Act - an offence to aid a suicide

☑ **STARMER GUIDELINES** - Clarified when prosecution was likely to occur (2013)

☑ Quality of Life arguments (eg Singer) in conflict with sanctity of life (Church)

☑ Kantian ethics can derive rational sanctity of life argument.

☑ Slippery slopes can be prevented by careful laws e g. Oregon rules (**USA**)

☑ Individual rights or communal rights?

Bonus Points

☑ "Euthanasia is a grave violation of the law of God." **JOHN PAUL II**, 1995

☑ Diane Pretty court case - European Court 2002 - ruled right to life of **ARTICLE** 1 did not include right to die

☑ **OREGON RULES** in **USA** give practical examples of how a slippery slope may be prevented in law (eg by requiring two doctors three weeks apart to give independent assessment of meant health)

☑ **DANIEL JAMES** (2008) in fear and loathing of his ordinary life after rugby accident

☑ Active euthanasia is legal in Switzerland (**DIGNITAS**) and since 2002, in Netherlands and Belgium

Scan me
for more help

Or type **i-pu.sh/S7Z58B08** into your browser

Overview

- ☑ Varied issues and methods

- ☑ Gene therapies find cures

- ☑ Genetic manipulation designs disease-free babies

- ☑ Recombinant **DNA** combines genes from different plants/animals (1972)

- ☑ Genetically modified seed is used to boost yields but cannot reproduce

- ☑ Insulin is an example of a human drug created by **GE**

- ☑ 1976 **GM** animals;1983 **GM** plants

Key Terms

GENES	*Inherited attributes encoded in four letters*
GENE THERAPY	*Treatment of diseases by genetic modification or implantation*
PREIMPLANTATION DIAGNOSIS	*Diagnose illnesses before embryo implant*
RECOMBINANT DNA	*Genetic material combined from two sources*
CLONING	*Copying the genetic structure of an organism eg Dolly the sheep*

Genetic Engineering

Meaning

☑ Be careful to define carefully which form of **GE**

☑ Film Gattaca illustrates a two-tier society of "perfect" and "imperfect."

☑ 1,300 conditions can be diagnosed genetically eg breast cancer

☑ Embryo research involves using stem-cells to grow new material

Strengths

⊕ **HEALTH BENEFITS** - New treatments eg of diabetes

⊕ **CHOICE** - Parents can choose to avoid inherited diseases in foetuses

⊕ **WELFARE** - **GM** crops greatly increase yields

Weaknesses

⊖ **UNKNOWN CONSEQUENCES** - Fears of upsetting the crop ecosystem

⊖ **GENETIC PURITY** - Arguments about two-tiers of human (Gattaca film)

⊖ **PLAYING GOD** - Making choices without forseeing implications. Dolly the sheep died young

Scan me
for more help

Or type **i-pu.sh/R7L66S35** into your browser

IVF Treatment & Right to a Child

Applied Ethics

Overview

- ☑ **IVF** treatments usually involve embryo wastage
- ☑ Designing babies is prohibited
- ☑ Uneven right to **IVF** cycles - Justice?
- ☑ Cost - Around £8,000 a cycle
- ☑ Age limited - At 37, right ceases
- ☑ Only 25% of attempts succeed.

Key Terms

IVF	*In Vitro Fertilisation or test-tube fertilisation*
EMBRYO	*Foetus at six days to eight weeks*
PRE-EMBRYO	*Foetus before six days*
CYCLE	*One attempt to fertilise human eggs in vitro*

IVF Treatment & Right to a Child

Meaning

☑ Should we have the right to choose the genetic makeup of our children?

☑ Is the right to have a child absolute or conditional on cost?

☑ Is infertility a medical condition?

☑ At present ethical test is applied to potential mothers by **NHS** ethics committees

☑ Natural Law theory suggests artificial manipulation of embryos a violation of "intrinsic essence" of an embryo

☑ 2008 Human Fertilisation and Embryology Act

Strengths

⊕ **CHOICE** - Parental choice extended

⊕ **INCLUSIVE** - Includes gay couples

⊕ **HAPPINESS** - Increased by more wanted babies

Weaknesses

⊖ **FAILURE** - Rates are high - 75% overall

⊖ **EXPECTATIONS** - Rise only to be dashed - a disutility

⊖ **SCARCE RESOURCES** - Wasted on non-medical procedures

Scan me
for more help

Or type **i-pu.sh/R6D36H57** into your browser

Overview

☑ A bacterium delivers **DNA** into the chromosomes of a host plant

☑ 1985 field trials began

☑ 1995 the slow softening tomato goes on sale

☑ Cotton, oil seed rape and corn are widely grown as **GM** crops in Africa

☑ 90% poor farmers

Key Terms

GM FOOD *Genetically modified to increase yields/give disease resistance*

BIODIVERSITY *Variety of natural plant life*

FRANKENSTEIN FOODS *Produced by genetic modification with unknown effects*

Genetically Modified Plants

Meaning

☑ Islamic Iran has adopted **GM** rice but Christian **UK** has so far banned **GM** crops - Is **GM** un-Christian?

☑ Power issues remain - Suicide rates of small famers in India linked to expense of **GM** crops and as seed cannot be resown, dependency rises. Is this unjust?

☑ Genes are patented for commercial benefit. Is this morally right?

Strengths

⊕ **FAMINE** - Avoided by increased yields

⊕ **WELFARE** - Farmers benefit from disease resistance

⊕ **INNOVATION** - New crops, new solutions

Weaknesses

⊖ **HEALTH RISKS** - Altered plant metabolism? Affects human metabolism

⊖ **EXPENSE** - Poor farmers cannot afford to replace seed

⊖ **BIODIVERSITY** - Declines as plant species destroyed by cross-fertilisation

Scan me
for more help

Or type **i-pu.sh/P6L22V42** into your browser

Overview

☑ **JUS AD BELLUM** - Right authority, Just cause, Just intention, Last resort, Reasonable chance of success, Proportionality

☑ **JUS IN BELLO** - Proportionality, Civilians protected, Military necessity

☑ **JUS POST BELLUM** - Just cause, right intention, Public declaration, Proportionality of surrender terms

Key Terms

JUS AD BELLUM   *When it is morally right to go to war*

JUS IN BELLO   *Moral conduct of war*

JUS POST BELLUM *Moral conditions for a just peace*

Just War Theory

Meaning

- ☑ Just war develops from Augustine/Aquinas/Suarez
- ☑ Taken up by Catholic Bishops in **US**
- ☑ Interpreted by Geneva Convention

Strengths

- ⊕ **MORAL GUIDELINES** are clear
- ⊕ **REALISTIC** - War is sometimes necessary
- ⊕ **UNIVERSAL** - Basis for Geneva Convention (1949)

Weaknesses

- ⊖ **RELATIVE** - To perspective eg Guantanomo Bay detainees
- ⊖ **AMBIGUOUS** - Conditions - what makes a "right authority eg in Syria?
- ⊖ **INAPPROPRIATE** to an age of global terrorism and state anarchy

Scan me
for more help

Or type **i-pu.sh/F1R06H15** into your browser

Overview

Bertrand Russell argued "that very few wars are worth fighting, and that the evils of war are almost always greater than they seem to excited populations at the moment when war breaks out" eg **WWII**.

John Rawls argues "the possibility of a just war is conceded but not under present circumstances."

Jus ad vellum - Contingent pacifists may reject the legitimacy of the authority or argue that war is not being fought as a last resort, or that the war is being fought for a just cause.

Jus in bello - They point to innocent noncombatants being harmed or that soldiers employing evil means (such as rape or torture).

Jus post vellum - Contingent pacifists may object to wars that will undermine long-term peace, justice and stability.

Key Terms

AHISMA	*Non violence*
ABSOLUTE PACIFISM	*Never right to use violence*
CONTINGENT PACIFISM	*Dependent on circumstances*

Pacifism

Meaning

ABSOLUTE - Absolutely wrong to kill the innocent even if unintended consequence.

Contingent pacifists argue killing in self-defence is always justified.

Rightness of war depends on circumstances.

Bertrand Russell opposed **WW**1 but saw rightness of fighting Nazism.

Strengths

✚ CONTINGENT PACIFISM

✚ CONSEQUENTIALIST - Considers effects of non-intervention)

✚ REALISTIC - About human nature and value if deterrence)

✚ CAUTIOUS - Strengthens jus ad bellum rules of war (eg last resort) in light of jus in bello considerations (eg protect the innocent)

Weaknesses

✚ PREDICTION IMPOSSIBLE - Of consequences

✚ PRAGMATIC - Seems to waver on the key principle of non-violence

Scan me
for more help

Or type **i-pu.sh/H0L23S07** into your browser

Overview

☑ Universal values apply everywhere for all time

☑ Objective values exist out there in the world eg Natural Law, in the God-designed nature (inclinations) of human beings and physical laws

☑ Categorical rules emerge not dependent on circumstances or consequences eg Natural Law

Key Terms

ABSOLUTISM *The view that values don't change in different circumstances*

UNIVERSAL *Values can be consistently observed every-where*

OBJECTIVE *Values can be empirically measured in the real world*

Absolutism

Meaning

☑ Either, we can use our pure reason to determine these absolutes; Or, there's a God who clearly commands these absolutes

☑ Values rise above culture and can be universally observed

Bonus Points

☑ Kantian ethics is the most absolute as it creates absolute commands called categoricals

☑ Natural law theory is interpreted as absolute by the **RC** church. But is it?

☑ "Absolute" is ambiguous between "absolute rule that can't be changed" and "universal rule that applies everywhere for all time."

Scan me
for more help

Or type **i-pu.sh/N5L92D16** into your browser

Overview

Cultural relativism is a descriptive theory - Different cultures (empirically) generate different values, "Values are socially-approved habits", Ruth Benedict.

Normative relativism argues there can be no universal, objective truths.

Relativism is an ambiguous term - It can mean particular to a culture, or consequentialist (relative to circumstances) or subjective (up to me).

Situation ethics is described by Joseph Fletcher as "principled relativism", with one principle, agape love.

Key Terms

CULTURAL RELATIVISM	*Descriptive fact that cultures produce different values*
NORMATIVE RELATIVISM	*There can be no objective truth*
DEPENDENCY THESIS	*View that all values depend on cultures*
DIVERSITY THESIS	*View that cultures inevitably show diversity of values*
EMOTIVISM	*Values are expressions of emotion*

Relativism

Meaning

Goodness can have no metaphysical or objective basis.

Values are just descriptions of how people behave, with a positive or negative opinion attached.

There is no way of judging between different views.

In meta-ethics, emotivism reflects this subjective view - Values are just 'expressions of emotion'.

Bonus Points

☑ Pope Benedict - "The tyranny of relativism"

☑ Veritatis Splendor (1995 Encyclical) targets relativism and subjectivism

☑ "There are no objective truths," **JL** Mackie - itself an absolute statement

☑ Situation Ethics is not pure relativism - One absolute value (love)

Scan me
for more help

Or type **i-pu.sh/G1B45G80** into your browser

Overview

☑ A Christian ethic stressing the importance of law

☑ Law includes the ten commandments and the teaching of Christ

☑ Law is revealed to us in the Bible which is "God-inspired" (2 Timothy 3:16)

☑ God's omniscience and omnibenevolence underpins the law

☑ "I am the Lord, abounding in steadfast love and compassion" (Exodus 34:6)

Key Terms

EUTHYPHRO'S DILEMMA	*Either something is good because God commands it or God commands it because it is good*
ABHORRENT COMMANDS	*God commands immoral acts such as the slaughter of the citizens of Jericho*
EMPTINESS PROBLEM	*If goodness exactly equals what God commands then it empties goodness of rational moral content*

Divine Command

Meaning

☑ An idea of biblical inspiration is implied by **DC** theory - literalism

☑ Commands cannot be culturally determined

☑ Commands have to be easy to understand. But are they?

☑ Commands have to be easy to apply. But are they?

☑ Anscombe argues that a **LEGALISTIC** view of ethics has placed the focus on obedience, verdicts and penalties rather than personal character and the Virtues. Without belief in God this makes no sense

Bonus Points

☑ Are commands as absolute as implied here? Thou shalt not kill? Self-defence?

☑ Biblical commands change eg Jesus is arguably a pacifist

☑ Some commands seem immoral eg Joshua is commanded to slaughter people of Jericho

☑ If commands depend on God's character (love, compassion) shouldn't we exercise our judgement?

☑ Philip Quinn is a modern day Divine Command Theorist

☑ Would Abraham have sinned if he'd refused to sacrifice Isaac? Aquinas argues so, because "the Lord of life and death commanded it."

Scan me
for more help

Or type **i-pu.sh/J8Z19W68** into your browser

Lightning Source UK Ltd.
Milton Keynes UK
UKOW07f0246170216

268533UK00010B/38/P